Album of Prehistoric Animals

By TOM McGOWEN

Illustrated by ROD RUTH

RAND McNALLY & COMPANY
Chicago · New York · San Francisco

Text and illustrations reviewed and
authenticated by Dr. William Turnbull
Curator of Fossil Mammals
Field Museum of Natural History
Chicago, Illinois

Library of Congress Cataloging in Publication Data

McGowen, Tom.
  Album of prehistoric animals.

  SUMMARY: A brief, general introduction to the
history and characteristics of prehistoric mammals in
general, and specific descriptions of twelve different
kinds.
  1. Mammals, Fossil—Juvenile literature. [1. Mammals, Fossil. 2. Prehistoric animals] I. Ruth, Rod,
illus. II. Title.
QE881.M337   569   74-8486
ISBN 0-528-82032-X
ISBN 0-528-82033-8 (lib. bdg.)

Contents

Mammals — THE FURRY BEASTS

SEVENTY MILLION years ago, a giant animal prowled through a hot, moist forest. From the tip of its long tail to its huge snout, it was nearly 50 feet in length, and its great head was nearly 20 feet above the ground. A tall man would have reached only to its knees. As the animal moved through the greenery, shafts of sunlight, slanting through the leaves, shimmered on the scales that covered the enormous body. For the creature was a reptile—a scaly-skinned reptile of the kind that have been named *dinosaurs*.

The world this dinosaur lived in was lit-erally a world of reptiles. Scores of different kinds of dinosaurs stalked and scampered and lumbered upon the land. In the seas were giant reptiles that resembled fish and legendary sea serpents. And in the air there were reptiles that flapped and soared on leathery wings. Reptiles were the "rulers" of the earth.

But as the giant dinosaur strode past a clump of ferns, a pair of bright little eyes gleamed out at it. An animal was hidden among the ferns—an animal that was com-pletely different from the dinosaur and every other reptile. It was a sharp-nosed,

8

EARLY MAMMALS

Ichthyornis

long-tailed, ratlike little beast with skin that was covered with hair instead of scales. Its whole body was not as long as one of the dinosaur's teeth, and the big reptile probably did not even notice it. But in a few million years, this insignificant little animal's descendants would be the new owners of the earth; and the dinosaurs and most of the other reptiles would be gone forever! For the little beast was a mammal— an ancestor of the great family of mammals that fills the world today. That family includes dogs, cats, horses, cows, camels, elephants, bears, dolphins, and *us*—human beings.

Tyrannosaurus Rex

How was it possible for these little furry beasts to take over the world from the dinosaurs? How was it possible for them to change into so many different things? The answer to that lies in the word *evolution*— the name we have given to the force of nature that causes living things to change slowly, over many millions of years, until they are completely different from their ancestors.

When an animal is changed by evolution, it is often made better able to survive than its ancestors were. Such was the case with mammals. The ancestors of the mammals were one group of *reptiles,* and the mammals were an improvement over them.

Reptiles have certain problems. For one thing, they are cold-blooded. This means their bodies get just as hot or as cold as the air around them. If a reptile is in a hot, sunny place, such as a desert, its body soaks up the heat. The reptile could get so hot that its blood would literally boil. The reptile must get rid of some of the heat by moving into shade or into water and staying there until it cools off. And if the air becomes cold, as often happens at night, the reptile's body cools off until the reptile becomes stiff and slow-moving. Then it must warm up by lying in sunshine until it can move easily again. Reptiles often have to spend a lot of time either cooling off or warming up!

Mammals don't have this problem. Their furry, warm-blooded bodies cool off or warm up automatically. When a mammal's body gets too hot, each hair lifts up so that air can reach the skin. Little glands in the skin—sweat glands—pull water out of the mammal's body. That water brings heat with it, and when the water evaporates, the heat is carried away and the mammal is cooled. On the other hand, in cold air a mammal's hair lies flat against the skin, holding in the body heat so that the mammal is kept warm.

Thanks to evolution a mammal doesn't have to lie still and wait to cool off or warm up as a reptile does. And this is a big improvement. A mammal can keep right on hunting for food, digging a shelter, or doing whatever it wants, while its body takes care of heat and cold automatically.

Another difference between mammals and reptiles is the way they're born and the way they get food as babies. Most reptile mothers lay eggs and then just wander away, leaving the eggs to hatch out by themselves. The eggs are usually unprotected. They can be eaten by animals, stepped on and crushed, covered up by sandstorms. If the eggs do hatch, the reptile babies must start right out hunting for food for themselves. They're on their own.

But again, the way mammals are born is an improvement. Mammal babies don't come out of eggs; they grow inside their mothers' bodies, safe and protected until they are born. Then, unlike reptile babies that have to start hunting food, mammal babies are fed by their mothers. The food of all baby mammals is milk that is made inside the mother's body and comes out of openings called *mammae.* It is from that word that the name *mammal* comes.

Of course, none of these differences came

Present-day Lizard

about quickly. The reptiles that were the mammals' ancestors changed a little at a time, over millions of years. First, their teeth and their digestive systems changed, so that they were able to chew their food better and get more energy from it. This helped them become warm-blooded. Their scales slowly changed to hairs, for that's what a hair is—a scale that has been changed by evolution. Sweat glands formed in their skins. Later, in some of the females, sweat glands evolved into milk glands—mammae. Most of these evolving creatures continued to lay eggs. But in time some stopped laying eggs. They gave birth to live young.

Those first "true" mammals—furry and warm-blooded and giving birth to live babies that they fed with milk—probably appeared in the world between 150 million and 100 million years ago. And this was right at the time when the great dinosaurs ruled the earth. So for millions of years mammals shared the swamps and forests with the dinosaurs. Those first kinds of mammals were tiny, ratlike beasts only a few inches long. They ate insects and probably fruit, seeds, buds, worms, and the flesh of dead animals they found. They probably weren't as smart or as quick moving as most of the mammals of today, but they were smarter and quicker than most reptiles, and well able to hold their own in a world that reptiles ruled.

Millions of years rolled by, and the Age of Reptiles came to an end. For reasons we don't know, the dinosaurs and other big reptiles died out. Now, the world became a good place for the little furry beasts. And evolution continued its work, changing them into many different forms. The Age of Mammals had begun.

The Age of Mammals has been going on for about 70 million years. Many different kinds of furry beasts have come and gone during all those years. You will read about some of those strange, ancient mammals in this book. We know a lot about these beasts, from their fossil skeletons and their similarities to modern mammals. But there are still many things we don't know for sure. The stories about the animals in this book are based on the beliefs of many scientists as to how the animals may have lived, but it's important to remember that many details of those beliefs are based on little more than guesswork. For many of those ancient mammals, such as the huge "thunder beast," the "shovel-tusked" elephant, and the puzzling Arsinoitherium, were not really quite like any animals living now. If it weren't for their fossil bones, preserved for millions of years, we might never have known that such creatures ever lived.

Oxyeana

Phenacodus — HERDS AND HOOFS

SIXTY MILLION years ago, most of the world was warm and tropical. Palm trees grew in the northern parts of North America, and crocodiles sunned themselves on warm river banks in green forests where barren, rock-filled deserts lie today.

In a lush, tropical forest spread out in part of what is today the state of Wyoming, a small herd of sheep-sized animals prowled in search of food. They looked like a mixture of cat and tapir, with long heads, short, heavy legs, and long, thick, pointed tails that dragged behind them on the ground—tails that were still a lot like the tails of reptiles. Each foot had five toes, with the middle toe longer than the others. On each toe was a blunt claw, like a small hoof.

This animal's name is *Phenacodus*. It was probably the first mammal in the world to live in herds. And it was one of the first animals in the world to have hoofs.

The beasts moved slowly, investigating the underbrush. When a low-growing, juicy-leafed plant was discovered, it was devoured, as were the pulpy fruits that had fallen to the ground from overhanging branches. When one of the animals came across a fuzzy caterpillar crawling labori-

ously upon a leaf, it ate leaf, caterpillar and all. Phenacodus did not scorn anything it could chew—not even the rotting flesh of other, dead animals.

A path, well worn by the feet of many creatures, wound through the part of the forest where the Phenacodus herd was browsing. The path led down to a river, and following it, the Phenacodus herd emerged from the trees after a while onto a broad, muddy bank. The bank was occupied by half a dozen, good-sized crocodiles that lay basking in the sun. Their scaly, yellowish-brown bodies were absolutely motionless, and their amber eyes were unwinking. The members of the Phenacodus herd knew better than to stray too near the placid-seeming reptiles, however, and bunched together, keeping wary eyes on the crocodiles as they made their way farther down the bank. They found a place that seemed safe and moved down to the water's edge to drink.

Out near the middle of the river, a group of cow-sized creatures were cavorting with great snorts and squeals. They looked somewhat like hippopotamuses. Their skins were smooth and their bodies were big and bulky, but their legs were quite short, with

Crocodiles

Coryphodons

broad, five-toed feet. Their heads were large and wide, and their tails were small and ropelike. Like hippopotamuses, they spent most of their time in the water and ate mostly water plants.

Although these animals were plant eaters, they had two sharp tusks, like the teeth of a flesh-eating animal, in both their upper and lower jaws. Those tusks were weapons; the animals sometimes had to fight to protect their young ones from the attacks of the predators that shared the river with them. Because of its tusks, this animal has been named *Coryphodon,* a name that means "pointed tooth."

There was a large clump of trees and bushes near the place where the Phenacodus herd was drinking, and another animal was crouching there, hidden from sight. It was about the size of a police dog and had an odd, half-dog, half-cat appearance, with a blunt head and long, rounded tail. It was a flesh eater named *Oxyeana,* and it was hungry. Much of the time it ate only the flesh of dead animals it found, but if it had the chance it would sometimes attack and kill smaller, defenseless beasts. Now it peered through the bushes at the Phenacodus herd and waited. If a Phenacodus came near enough, the Oxyeana would leap out at it.

But the flesh eater was in for a disappointment. Another hungry animal was already moving toward the Phenacodus herd, unseen by them, or by the Oxyeana or the coryphodonts. It moved as silently as a shadow, only the tips of its nostrils and the bumps of its eyes showing above the water.

It was a large crocodile that had singled out a half-grown Phenacodus standing ankle-deep in the water.

The Phenacodus hardly knew what happened. Its snout, poking down into the water, was suddenly seized in the cruel grip of the crocodile's jaws. There was a flurry of splashes as the big reptile carried its floundering prey out into deeper water, spinning itself through the water with a powerful twisting movement that quickly broke the Phenacodus's neck and nearly tore its head loose from its body.

The sudden splashes startled the rest of the Phenacodus herd into instant flight. With ungainly bounds they dashed back into the safety of the forest. The Oxyeana, crouched in its hiding place, leaped to its feet and took a few halfhearted steps after them, but it was much too late and far too slow to give chase. It stared stupidly at the part of the forest into which they had vanished, then turned and trotted off to seek a meal somewhere else.

These three creatures—Phenacodus, Oxyeana, and Coryphodon—were typical of the kinds of mammals that filled the world in the earliest days of the Age of Mammals, the age that began with the extinction of the dinosaurs and the takeover of the world by furry, warm-blooded animals.

The dinosaurs and the other big reptiles that shared the world with them all died out about 65 million years ago. For the most part, only little creatures were left in the land—insects, frogs and toads, lizards, birds, and the little ratlike mammals.

The mammals could eat anything—insects, nuts, fruits, seeds, leaves, worms, and the meat of dead animals they found. And, except for snakes, crocodiles, and a few kinds of large birds, they had few enemies to prey on them regularly. When an animal has plenty of food and few enemies to keep it in check, it can multiply. The mammals spread out, rapidly.

And many of them began to get bigger. This couldn't have happened when the dinosaurs were around; any mammals that had gotten big enough to be noticed by the flesh-eating dinosaurs would have been quickly wiped out. But with the dinosaurs gone, there was nothing to stop the mammals. So by the time about five million years had passed, mammals had evolved into many different kinds. Some stayed small, others had grown big. Some still ate almost anything, some were beginning to eat nothing but plants, and some—the carnivores—were eating nothing but meat.

Phenacodus, Oxyeana, and Coryphodon were typical of those early beasts. Compared to the mammals of today, they were awkward and clumsily built, with thick bodies and tails, and big feet. And they were rather dull witted, with small, reptile-like brains. In some ways—their small brains, their long, heavy tails, their toes—they were still much like their reptile ancestors.

Phenacodus, Oxyeana, and Coryphodon belonged to mammal families that have been gone from the earth for many millions of years. There is nothing quite like them living today.

Phenacodus was a condylarth. It was a kind of "in-between" animal, for it was somewhat like the sharp-toothed flesh eaters of its time, yet it seems to have been a plant eater that was developing hoofs and living in herds.

Coryphodon was an amblypod, named "blunt foot." In size and shape, and judging from where its fossils have been found, it was probably much like a hippopotamus.

Oxyeana was a creodont, which means "flesh tooth." Although it probably looked much like a dog, it was not at all related to dogs or wolves. It belonged to a family of beasts that has been gone from the earth for millions of years.

Coryphodon

Oxyeanas

Arsinoitherium — THE MYSTERY MAMMAL

IN THE SHADE of a clump of bushes that grew on a broad, grassy plain spreading across part of Egypt 50 million years ago, a baby animal was awakening to its second day of life. It lay beneath the bushes with its legs folded under its body. The pudgy animal was about the size of a full-grown pig.

The baby's mother stood protectively over it. She was a huge, bulky animal, 11 feet long and nearly 6 feet high at the shoulders, about the size of a present-day rhinoceros. She looked somewhat like a rhinoceros, too. But instead of having a long, slim horn on her nose, she had two enormous, thick horns that grew side by side out of her forehead and projected straight out above her nose. This heavy-horned animal is called *Arsinoitherium.*

The baby Arsinoitherium had done nothing but eat and sleep during the first 24 hours of its life, but now it was growing stronger and able to accompany its mother for short distances as she traveled about in search of food and water. So when the mother moved a few steps away, to pull a mouthful of leaves from one of the bushes, the baby stood up to follow. On still-shaky legs it wobbled to her side, pushed its head

against her belly, and found the place where its food came from. Hungrily, it sucked a meal of rich, warm milk.

After a time, the mother Arsinoitherium started off across the plain toward a long line of distant trees and shrubs that marked the course of a river. The baby, gaining strength, trotted close at her side. Whenever she stopped to investigate a smell, or to nibble at some juicy leaves on a low-growing plant, the baby would push its head under her body for a milky snack.

When they reached the river, the mother Arsinoitherium waded a few steps into the water and began to drink her fill. The baby stayed close behind her. It was nervous and somewhat frightened now, for here at the river there were many new things for it to see and hear and smell.

The baby watched fearfully as, a short distance away, a small group of pig-sized animals, their bodies glistening wetly, emerged from the water and clambered up onto the bank. Their bodies were long; their legs were short, with blunt, five-toed feet; and their heads were narrow and long-snouted, with flexible noses that curled down over their mouths. Each one had two small, sharp tusks in both upper and lower

Hyaenod

Moeritherium

Aegyptopithecus

jaws. These smallish creatures certainly looked nothing at all like elephants—but that's what they were evolving toward. As a matter of fact, these animals, called *Moeritherium,* were the ancestors of all the kinds of elephants that have ever lived.

A sudden frenzied chattering from overhead made the baby Arsinoitherium press closer to its mother's leg. A group of apelike creatures that lived among the trees along the river bank were having a disagreement, screaming with anger and pelting each other with twigs. These chattering creatures, called *Aegyptopithecus,* may have been the ancestors of apes—and of people!

The mother Arsinoitherium paid no attention to any of these goings-on. Neither Moeritherium nor Aegyptopithecus was any threat to her or her baby. As a matter of fact, with her big, strong body and fierce horns, she was safe from the attacks of most animals.

But as she finished her drink and turned away from the water, she saw something that brought a deep rumble of anger from her throat. For here *was* danger—not to herself, but to her baby!

A number of large, doglike creatures were trotting toward the river. These animals belonged to a family of mammals known as *Hyaenodon,* and they were flesh eaters, much like the African hyenas of today. They were willing to eat anything, including meat from the bones of dead animals they chanced to find. And they would attack and pull down any small animal, or the young of large ones, that couldn't defend itself—animals such as the baby Arsinoitherium.

The hyaenodonts stopped, clustered together, and stared toward the mother and her young one. They were like a gang of bullies trying to decide whether to pick a fight. The big Arsinoitherium watched them angrily, rumbling all the while. Sensing the danger, the baby huddled close against her.

Had the hyaenodonts been hungry, the baby Arsinoitherium's life might have come to an end then and there. For despite the mother's terrible horns and the broad, heavy feet that could crush another animal to jelly, the hyaenodonts might have made an attempt to separate her from the baby. Some of them would have begun to encircle her, as if to come at the baby from behind, and had she angrily charged those, others would have quickly moved in and killed the helpless young one.

But mother and baby Arsinoitherium were in luck, for the hyaenondonts had just finished gobbling up the remains of a dead animal they had found, and were coming to the river only to drink. After staring at the mother Arsinoitherium for a time, several of the doglike beasts turned away as if no longer interested and trotted down to the water. The others followed.

Quickly, the mother Arsinoitherium swung toward her little one. With her nose and horns she pushed it into a trot, nudging it along ahead of her as they moved away from the river and back out onto the broad prairie.

After a time, the river and its dangers

Hyaenodon

were far behind them. The mother stopped and began to browse among some bushes that offered a meal of tasty leaves. Nudging its way beneath her, the baby, too, began to feed with great contentment.

The sun, which had risen high in the sky, slowly began to slide back down, spreading afternoon warmth over the great plain. The mother Arsinoitherium turned away from the bushes. Ponderously she sank to the ground with her legs tucked beneath her. The baby, tired from the excitement and activity of its first real taste of life, nestled beside her, yawning repeatedly until it fell asleep with its chin resting on the ground. Soon both animals were dozing side by side in the hot sunshine, their ears twitching and turning, listening even while they slept. The slightest sound that might mean danger would arouse them at once to wakefulness.

The fossil skeleton of Arsinoitherium was first discovered in 1900. It was a mystery animal for scientists then, and it's just as much of a mystery today. For no one can figure out what *kind* of an animal Arsinoitherium was. Although it may have looked much like a modern rhinoceros, it wasn't even distantly related to the rhinoceros family. The fact is, we're not sure *what* animal it may be related to. It doesn't seem to belong to any of the animal families, ancient or modern, that have ever existed. We don't know what its ancestors were like, and we don't know if it left any descendants.

But there may be one clue. In Africa and parts of southwestern Asia there lives a little animal called a hyrax. It's about the size of a rabbit and it looks a lot like a guinea pig. This little animal's teeth and the teeth of Arsinoitherium are very much alike. Certain parts of their skeletons are also alike. Could the huge, bulky, big-horned Arsinoitherium of 50 million years ago be related to the tiny, scampering, furry hyrax of today? Some scientists think so; others say there's no basis for such a notion.

So we just don't know what Arsinoitherium was. The answer, if there is one, may lie with some future discovery. Until then, Arsinoitherium will continue to be one of the most mysterious of all the mammals.

Present-day Rock Hyrax

Eohippus — THE DAWN HORSE

IT WAS DAWN over the North America of 55 million years ago. At the eastern horizon, the red morning sun was creeping into the sky, driving out night's blackness and covering up the stars. As the ruddy light moved across them, the green, swampy forests and rolling uplands waked into life. Bird voices screeched, twittered, and quacked. Insects, warmed into activity after the night's coolness, filled the air with chirps, creaks, and buzzes. The creatures of the night retreated into their dens and holes, and the creatures of day set out upon the important business of finding food.

In a broad glade in a great forest, a herd of animals had begun their morning feeding. They were dainty creatures, no bigger than house cats, with slender legs and little feet with spreading toes. There were four toes on their front feet, and three on the back ones, and on each toe was a tiny hoof. The animals' tails were longish and stout, and their backs were high and curved, like the backs of rabbits. Their heads were rather deerlike. They certainly didn't look much like horses. But that's what they were —the first true horses, ancestors of the horses of today. Their official name is *Hyracotherium*, but many people prefer to

call them by the name *Eohippus*, which means "dawn horse."

Modern horses are grazers, grass eaters. But there wasn't much grass in the world of 55 million years ago, and even if there had been, little Eohippus couldn't have eaten it, for its teeth weren't strong enough to chew such tough vegetation. These first little horses were browsers that lived in forests and fed on soft, juicy leaves, tender buds, and pulpy fruits.

Hours passed and the sun slowly rose higher. The little horses had nearly finished their feeding. Shortly, they would troop to the nearest pool for a long, satisfying drink. Then they would seek places in the deep shade of the woods, where they would lie hidden until the forest became filled with late afternoon shadows. The horses would come forth to browse again for a while in the hours before sundown.

Suddenly, from out of the forest that surrounded the glade, a pair of monsters emerged. They strode on two powerful legs that ended in sharp-taloned three-toed feet with heel-like back appendages. Red eyes gleamed, and wickedly curved beaks jutted out of their big, feathered heads. They were giant birds, taller than a tall man, and they

Diatryma

20

Eohippus   Orohippus   Mesohippus   Merychippus   Present-day Horse

were flesh-eating killers.

At the first glimpse of these two enemies, the horses exploded into flight, rushing in terror for the far end of the glade. They moved swiftly—but the giant birds could move swiftly, too. Their wings were useless for flying, but their legs were made for running. Feet drumming on the ground, they sped after the horses, their bodies bent far forward and their small wings spread out for balance. A sharp beak stabbed out savagely, closing around a little horse's back. The bird that had made a successful catch stopped and began to eat. The other bird pursued the horses on into the forest. . . .

Eohippus and the giant bird, which is called *Diatryma,* were both natives of the western part of North America, about where the states of Wyoming and New Mexico are today. But Eohippus wasn't strictly an American animal; fossil skeletons of these little creatures have been found in Europe, too.

But although we know very little about Eohippus's ancestor, we know a great deal about its descendants. The history of the horse family is probably the best known of all animal histories and is one of the best proofs of evolution, the process that causes animals to change their shapes and ways of life over many millions of years.

About 10 million years or so after the time of Eohippus came a horse that has been named *Orohippus.* It was a little larger than the cat-sized Eohippus, its head was more horselike in appearance, and its teeth were different. But it still had toes on its feet, as Eohippus did. When Orohippus first appeared on the scene, it lived in swampy forests, but near the end of its time on earth it moved out onto the grassy plains that were gradually taking over large parts of the world. It probably was beginning to eat grass instead of leaves.

Ten million more years passed, and the land changed. Most of the swampy forests had dried up and vanished completely, and enormous grass-filled plains now covered much of North America. A descendant of Eohippus called *Mesohippus* lived at this time. It was about the size of a police dog and looked much more like a horse than either of its ancestors, Eohippus or Orohippus, had. All of its feet had three toes with hoofs on them, but the middle toes and hoofs were much larger than the others. Mesohippus was becoming a one-toed animal like the modern horse. And, like the modern horse, it was strictly a grass eater.

Another 10 million or so years later—about 25 million years from our time—came *Merychippus,* which was about the size of a calf. Merychippus still had three toes on each foot, but two of the toes had become small, while on each foot the middle toe and its hoof had grown longer and much larger. The result was that Merychippus walked on only one toe on each foot, just as modern horses do, for its other side toes didn't even touch the ground. Merychippus probably looked so much like a modern horse that had you seen it galloping across an ancient prairie you might have said, "Look at the little pony!"

With the passage of many millions of

Evolution of Forefoot

Eohippus   Merychippus   Present-day Horse

years more, horses grew slowly larger while their useless "leftover" toes continued to become smaller. Finally, about a million years ago, the kind of horse we now have appeared in the world.

All this took place in North America. The little European Eohippus had a number of descendants, too, but for some reason they all died off. By about 30 million years ago there were no horses of any kind in Europe.

Thirty million years ago, North America was an island continent, entirely surrounded by water, as Australia is now. But off and on during the millions of years between that time and this one, earthquakes and volcanoes caused "land bridges" to push up out of the ocean. These bridges connected the western part of North America to Asia, and the southern part of North America to South America. Horses migrated over the bridges west into Asia and Europe and south into Central and South America. (A lot of other kinds of animals used the bridges, too). So horses reappeared in Europe and began to do very well there. They also seemed to be doing very well in South America.

Then about 25 thousand years ago, something mysterious happened in North and South America. All the horses in those countries—and a number of other kinds of animals, as well—became extinct. Why this happened is a puzzle that scientists have not been able to figure out. But at any rate, there were no horses left anywhere in the western hemisphere. About 500 years ago Spanish explorers brought horses with them from Europe, and so horses were reintroduced into the western world.

Since the time of little Eohippus, 55 million years ago, there have been herds of wild horses by the millions, often on several different continents at the same time. Today, the zebras of Africa, small herds of wild asses, and a very small group of Asiatic horses (called Pryzcwalski's Horse) are the only wild descendants left of the little dawn horse. There are probably just a few hundred thousand of these wild members of the horse family, altogether. Although there are many other horses in the world, they are all tame creatures that have become the servants of an animal that wasn't even around in Eohippus's day—the animal called man.

Brontotherium — THE THUNDER BEAST

THOUSANDS OF YEARS ago, when bands of Indians hunted among the hills and prairies of what is now South Dakota and Nebraska, they sometimes came across huge bones lying in gullies and ravines. The bones were not those of any animal the Indians had ever seen; they were far too big and thick to belong to even so large a beast as a bison. Usually, the bones were found only after there had been a heavy downpour of rain, so the Indians felt that rainstorms were somehow responsible for the bones being there.

A legend grew that the bones belonged to huge animals that lived in the sky. The Indians believed that the animals leaped down to earth during rainstorms, and that thunder was the sound of their big hoofs thudding into the ground when they landed. The Indians called these legendary beasts "thunder horses."

The bones were really fossil bones, of course—bones of real animals that had lived many millions of years ago. Heavy rains sometimes washed the bones out of their resting places in the sides of ravines, which was why they were usually found only after severe storms. But the Indians had no way of knowing about such things

as fossils. When the great fossil hunter Professor Othniel Marsh discovered many of these bones nearly a century ago, he remembered the old Indian legend of the thunder horses, and he named the prehistoric animal *Brontotherium,* which means "thunder beast."

The thunder beast was a massive, hulking animal. A tall man's head would not have reached to its shoulders. It was a good 8 feet high and nearly 15 feet long. It had thick, heavy legs and broad, spread-out feet to support the weight of a big, bulky body that weighed more than that of most elephants. Its rhinoceroslike head was rather small for such a massive body.

On its nose, the thunder beast had a thick, blunt horn, shaped like the letter **Y**. It used that horn in many ways. It undoubtedly fought other brontotheres to prove its superiority. It probably fought to defend its territory. And it may have used its heavy horn to protect its youngsters from the prowling, wolflike flesh eaters that were around in those days. To use its horn, the big beast must have lowered its head, nose to the ground, so that the horn jutted straight out. Then, with big feet drumming on the ground and

BRONTOTHERIUM

Poëbrotheriur

big body moving with surprising speed, it charged. The flesh eater that couldn't scramble out of the way in time was lifted up on the horn, and tossed high into the air with enough force to smash its bones when it hit the ground. Male brontotheres probably also used their horns to fight each other at times, too. Their horns were bigger than those of the females.

Today, the land through which the thunder beast once roamed has become wheat-filled farmland, pasture, and eroded ridges of clay and sandstone. But when the brontotheres were alive, they ambled about on moist, grassy plains dotted with water holes and dense clumps of trees and bushes. Surrounding the plains were mountain ridges, among which the cones of volcanoes often pointed upward at the sky.

Above one of the volcanoes that overlooked such a plain, on a day more than 40 million years ago, there hung a great, umbrella-shaped cloud of black, almost solid-looking smoke. From time to time the volcano rumbled ominously. The animals that made their home on the plain were restless, as if they sensed that the rumbles were a warning of danger that might leap out upon them at any moment. A large herd of three-toed horses the size of police dogs browsed upon the plain, as did a herd of sheep-sized, humpless camels. Doglike and catlike flesh eaters prowled in the tall grass or lay in ambush among the thickets.

In one of the many water holes, a group of brontotheres were soaking themselves, enjoying the coolness of the water on their tough, thick hides. A few of the big animals were nosing about in the bushes at the edge of the hole, seeking soft, juicy leaves of the kind that were their main food.

Suddenly, there was a sound—a muffled roar that slowly grew louder, like the noise of a swiftly approaching subway train. The ground beneath the brontotheres' feet began to quiver and shake. Then there was an ear-splitting explosion from the volcano. The entire plain shuddered violently, throwing even the big brontotheres to their knees. Red flames shot up from the volcano's cone, and the black cloud of smoke began to spread out over the plain, blotting out the sun, turning the sky as dark as a moonless night.

A shower of hot, wet ashes and chunks of steaming rock began to pour down upon the plain, hurled out of the volcano by the explosion. A sharp stench of burning sulfur filled the air. Confused and excited by the noise and the bits of rock pelting them, the brontotheres charged out of the water and milled about, bellowing.

With a titanic blast, the volcano blew itself into fragments. Out of the crater that was left poured a great, glowing, fiery flood that rushed down toward the plain—*liquid rock* from the earth's interior, rock so hot that it boiled and flowed like thick syrup! The plain that had been veiled in blackness moments before now became lit with a hellish orange glare.

At the sight of the river of fire rolling toward them, the animals of the plain bolted in terror. Plant eaters and flesh eaters ran side by side, their enmity forgotten in the face of the thing they all feared most of all. The brontotheres, too, were overcome with terror and joined the other creatures in flight. Big feet thudding, they galloped wildly in search of safety. . . .

The time during which the brontotheres lived was one of volcanic activity. That doesn't mean that volcanoes erupted every year, or even every 10 or 20 years. But we do know that there were volcanic eruptions where brontotheres lived, and the big beasts must have sometimes been terrorized by them.

Brontotheres, often known as titanotheres, meaning "giant beasts," descended from a little animal about the size of a small dog. Descendants of that small creature got bigger and bigger.

Brontotheres were the biggest members of the family, but they were also the last, because all the brontotheres living in North America and Asia died out about 35 million years ago. That was the end of the *Titanotherium* family. You could hardly call them "successful" animals, because they were around for only about 20 million years. That may seem like a long time, but

it isn't really. Many mammal families, such as horses, camels, and elephants, have been going strong for more than 50 million years. And turtles, horseshoe crabs, and many other kinds of creatures have been around for *hundreds* of millions of years.

It's hard to say why the thunder beasts became extinct. Some scientists think they may have been slow witted. But other even more slow-witted animals than they have survived. The last of the thunder beasts lived at a time when the climate was becoming drier, and grass was spreading through the world, crowding out the soft, leafy plants that needed lots of moisture, and that were the brontotheres' food. Perhaps the big beasts just couldn't adapt quickly enough to this change.

There is no animal quite like the thunder beast or any of the other titanotheres anywhere today. They were distantly related to horses, rhinoceroses, and tapirs, but were nevertheless a completely different kind of animal. And when they became extinct, their kind of animal was gone from the world forever.

Rhinoceros

Tapir

Comparative Size of Brontotherium and Present-day Animals

Platybelodon — THE SHOVEL-TUSKER

A GROUP of American scientists searching for fossils in the Gobi Desert of central Asia, in the year 1928, encountered a mystery. They found two large, flat, oblong-shaped objects, each about eight inches wide and half an inch thick. They appeared to be ivory, like the tusk of an elephant.

The scientists examined the things for a time and decided that they were teeth. But what kind of animal could have had such strange, huge, flat teeth?

During the weeks that followed the first discovery of the teeth, others were found, but never with any bones or any other clues as to the kind of beast they had belonged to. Then, one afternoon when the head of the expedition was returning to camp, he stumbled over something. Looking down, he saw a bit of one of the flat objects sticking up out of the ground.

He squatted down and began to chip away at the soft rock. Once again, there were two of the teeth, but this time they weren't by themselves—they were imbedded in a bone. Perhaps the mystery could now be solved.

With the help of the other men, the bone was freed from its age-old resting place. The scientists recognized it at once as a jawbone. But what a jawbone! It was about 5 feet long, and the two flat teeth were sticking straight out from the end of it, side by side. It looked like an enormous shovel!

Farther back on each side of the jaw were rows of big teeth that the scientists recognized at once. Those teeth showed that the animal to which the jaw had belonged was a mastodon.

Mastodons were big, elephantlike creatures. There had been several different kinds in the prehistoric world. But this mastodon with a jaw like a shovel was a new discovery.

The scientists were unable to find out more about it at this time, however, as they had to pack up and return to the United States. But two years later the expedition returned to the Gobi Desert, and almost at once the men began finding large quantities of fossil bones of the shovel-tusked mastodon—more jawbones, as well as other parts of skeletons. And from those bones and the place where they were found, the scientists were able to puzzle out the story of an ancient tragedy.

About 20 million years ago, in the place

where all the fossil bones were found, there had been a broad, deep lake that bulged at one end to form a small bay. Unlike the rest of the lake, which sent waves splashing in upon its beach, the waters of the sheltered bay were smooth and quiet. A mass of water lilies and other plants covered its surface. Cattails and bulrushes lined its shores.

At the water's edge, a large gray animal stood in the shallows up to its knees. From its little ropelike tail to its mouth, it was just about the size and shape of an elephant. But instead of an elephant's drooping, V-shaped mouth and long, round trunk, this creature had an enormously long, shovel-shaped lower jaw upon which rested a broad, flattened-out trunk. Two short, sharp tusks pointed out on each side of the trunk, and at the end of the lower jaw were two broad, flat tusks that stuck straight out to form the front of the "shovel."

The beast was feeding. It lowered its head toward the water and opened its mouth in a tremendous gape. With a forward movement of its head, it shoveled its long lower jaw through the water, scooping up a great, dripping mass of water lilies, roots and all. Its flat trunk curled down and back, shoving the wad of plants into the big mouth. Lifting its head, the beast began to chew, slowly and solemnly.

The shovel-tusked mastodon was not alone at the edge of the bay; there was a small herd of the great creatures standing in the shallow water. They had just discovered the bay in the course of their wander-

ings. It took a lot of food to fill those big gray bellies—hundreds of pounds a day—and the herd had been feeding since sunup, moving slowly through the great carpet of water lilies, their shovel-jaws scooping like big dredges. But now most of them were nearly satisfied. A few were making their way slowly toward dry ground.

However, the shovel-tusker chewing the batch of water lilies it had just dredged up was not quite comfortably full yet. It swallowed its mouthful and rolled its eyes downward, regarding the water in which it stood. The lilies were rather sparse there, but farther out in deeper water there were great inviting clusters of them. The shovel-tusker turned its big body and waded out until the water was up over its belly. Again, the long jaw dipped down and shoveled up a tangle of green stems and white flowers.

Most of the other members of the herd had climbed up onto shore and were plodding toward a nearby thicket where they would spend the hottest part of the day dozing in the shade. But the shovel-tusker in the water was still concerned with packing more food into itself. It took another few steps into the deeper water, not realizing that the mud beneath its feet was getting much softer and that it was sinking more deeply into it with each step.

Another load of lilies went into the beast's mouth. It munched contentedly, then swallowed. Again the big mouth yawned open, the long jaw dipped into the water. The beast waded a few more steps. And suddenly, it was floundering. For this part of the bay dropped away abruptly into

30

a great hole, 40 feet deep and filled with thick, sticky mud.

Had it been water, the shovel-tusker might have been able to swim to safety, but the ooze into which its body was sinking was like glue! It was hopelessly trapped. The weight of its big body was pulling it slowly down into the seemingly bottomless hole. This is just the sort of thing that sometimes happens even today when a big-bodied animal such as an elephant or rhinoceros becomes mired in the ooze of a deep water hole.

The trapped shovel-tusker threshed about, trumpeting in panic. Its squeals attracted the attention of the rest of the herd, and they came hurrying back to shore to see what was happening.

That was the story the scientists in the Gobi Desert pieced together from the bones they found—bones of shovel-tusked mastodons piled in hard, green clay that had once been loose clinging mud. Perhaps some members of the herd had tried to help their mired comrade, as elephants do today, and they, too, were captured by the treacherous mud, for it was clear that many of the shovel-tuskers had fallen prey to the mud hole. Altogether, the scientists found the bones of 20 of the big animals in the green clay.

The shovel-tusked mastodon has been named *Platybelodon,* which means "flat frontal tooth." Descendants of Platybelodon wandered across the narrow bridge of land that connected Asia with North America 20 million years ago, and became Americans. They spread through the western part of the United States and Canada. About 14 million years ago, a shovel-tusker by the name of *Amebelodon* lived where the states of Kansas and Nebraska are today. Amebelodon's shovel-tusked jaw was 6 or 7 feet long—longer than a tall man's whole body.

There is nothing like these curious shovel-tusked creatures in the world now. Like so many of the other prehistoric mammals, all the shovel-tuskers died out many millions of years ago. Only the elephants are left today to give us a hint of what these strange, wonderful beasts were like.

Present-day Asia   Present-day North America

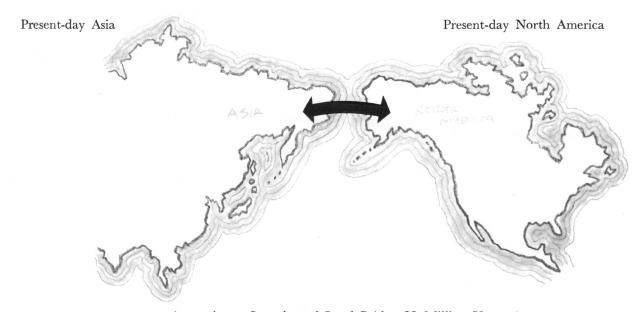

Approximate Location of Land Bridge 20 Million Years Ago

Alticamelus — THE GIRAFFE-CAMEL

IF SOMEONE asked you to name a desert animal, you would probably say "camel" without a moment's hesitation. And the camel is, undeniably, a true creature of the desert—a spindle-legged, knobby-kneed, humpbacked beast that is completely at home in the hot, sandy wastes of North Africa and the Near East, or the cold, dry deserts of northern Asia.

But camels weren't always desert dwellers. Ten million years ago, there wasn't a single camel on any desert in the world. Nor was there a single camel anywhere in Africa, Arabia, or any of the places where camels are now so plentiful. The only place you could have found camels 10 million years ago was on the plains and what is now the gulf coast of North America—the continent where the whole camel family began.

As a matter of fact, several different kinds of camels lived in North America 10 million years ago. And one of them was about as different from any camel living today as you can imagine. . . .

The sun shone down on a great, golden, grassy plain that spread out where Colorado and several other western states now lie. Trotting across the plain toward a

water hole lined with trees came a group of tall, gawky beasts with stiltlike legs and incredibly long, skinny necks. The heads at the ends of those necks were nearly 18 feet off the ground. The animals resembled giraffes in size and general shape, and they had no humps on their backs. Nevertheless they were camels—a kind of camel called *Alticamelus,* which means "high camel." Because of their strong resemblance to giraffes, they are also often called "giraffe-camels."

The giraffe-camels slowed to a walk and sauntered the last few yards to the water, heads nodding on long necks. Reaching the water's edge, they bent their heads to drink. A giraffe cannot do this without spreading its legs far apart because its neck is not quite long enough for its head to reach the ground, but for the giraffe-camel this was an easy matter.

Finishing its drink, one of the camels became interested in the leaves of a nearby tree. Modern camels browse on low-growing plants, but the giraffe-camel's neck enabled it to poke its nose among the branches of trees and feed on leaves that were out of the reach of most other plant eaters. Soon, the trees were filled with

32

Aelurodons

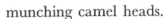

munching camel heads.

Abruptly, one of the animals snorted. Backing up a few steps, it pulled its head from the leaves and turned, facing the prairie. Nothing could be seen but waving grass tops, but the camel's nostrils flared as it tested the air. For just an instant while it had been eating, a scent—a sharp, animal smell—had filled its nose.

There it was again, strong and steady, carried by the breeze that had shifted direction and was now blowing in toward the water hole. The camel snorted again, suddenly nervous and uncertain, and now the other members of the little herd were alerted, too. With little, dancing steps they moved away from the trees, staring about.

Three wolflike creatures that had been slowly creeping through the grass toward the camels now abandoned caution and raced to the attack. Instantly, the camels bolted, galloping away with surprising speed on their long, spindly legs.

But one of the camels was cut off; a flesh eater had managed to get between it and the path to safety. With lips pulled back in a snarl that bared savage teeth, the flesh eater launched itself in a leap that was designed to bring it smashing into the camel's side, where it could fasten its teeth in the tall animal's neck and drag it to the ground.

But the camel had a surprise for its foe. Instinctively it twisted, reared on its hind legs, and lashed out with its front feet. The two big, pointed toes on one of the feet smacked into the wolflike creature's chest. The flesh eater gave a shrieking yelp of pain and shock as the force of the kick sent it

tumbling to the ground with smashed ribs and a ghastly deep slash across its chest. The other two wolflike animals stopped in their tracks, suddenly wary of those dangerous toes. Instantly, the giraffe-camel was galloping away.

Giraffe-camels were not the ancestors of the camels that live in the world today. They were offshoots of the camel family that flourished for a time, then died out and left no descendants. But the creature that scientists think *was* the ancestor of today's camels was living in North America at about the same time as the giraffe-camels. It was a smaller animal than the giraffe-camel and looked very much like the llamas that live in South America today. It has been named *Procamelus,* a word that means "before camel," showing that, while it wasn't quite a true camel, it was the last ancestor in line before the true camels began.

There are many questions connected with the camel family. If camels began in North America, how did they end up in Africa and Asia? How did they change from plains dwellers to desert animals? And why aren't there any camels in North America now?

It all came about this way. At about the time when Procamelus and the giraffe-camel were trotting about on the North American prairies, many kinds of animals were beginning to move into Asia and South America, and animals from South America and Asia were moving into North America. This couldn't happen before, because North America was separated from both

34

Procamelus

Asia and South America by miles and miles of water. But over a long period of time, earthquakes and volcanic eruptions had pushed up chunks of land out of the water, forming land connections to Asia and South America in two places. One of these places was between where Alaska and Mongolia, in Asia, are today. That land bridge is now broken—only a few little islands remain to show where it once was. The other place was where Panama, in Central America, joined Colombia, in South America. That bridge still exists.

Over these land bridges, some of the Procamelus herds slowly spread into Asia and South America. The South American llamas, alpacas, and vicunas of today are all descendants of those ancient wanderers that traveled south. And the Arabian and Bactrian camels that live in Asia and the Near East today are descendants of American camels that headed west.

The camels that moved into South America didn't change very much between then and now, except to grow thick coats of fur to keep them warm in the cold air of the high mountains where they finally settled. In fact, the South American guanaco, a kind of wild llama, looks almost exactly as its ancestors did.

But the camels that moved into Asia changed quite a bit. They found themselves in dry lands with few plants and little water. They had to learn to eat tough, dry, desert shrubs, and to go without water for long periods. Their bodies evolved in ways that helped them live in desert conditions. Mats of hair grew inside their ears to keep out the blowing sand, and their eyelids grew thick lashes for the same reason. They became able to close their nostrils completely when they had to. And they often had to go for days without food, so their bodies became able to store up fat in big humps on their backs—fat that their bodies could live on when there was no food. In short, those camels became what they are today—desert animals.

And what became of the camels that stayed in North America? For some reason, they all died off. In North America, the land where camels began and where they once roamed by the thousands, the only camels to be found today are those that have been brought from other countries to live in zoos.

Guanaco   Dromedary Camel   Bactrian Camel

Comparative Size of Alticamelus and Present-day Animals

Smilodon — THE SABER-TOOTHED CAT

A MILLION years ago, the western part of the United States was as filled with animals as a game preserve in Africa is today. Herds of horses, humpless camels, and big elephants with curved tusks roamed the yellow-green plains, where they were hunted by big cats and packs of pony-sized wolves. Great, shaggy ground sloths lumbered among the thickets, and giant beavers the size of small bears skillfully built dams in streams and rivers. Huge vultures perched in the trees, scanning the countryside with sharp, red eyes. They were waiting for some animal to kill another and eat its fill, after which they would move in on the dead carcass and pick its bones clean.

A number of these animals were moving about near a small water hole early one afternoon. Camels, elephants, and sloths were all minding their own business and intent only on filling their stomachs with the grass, leaves, or other plants that were their food. Unknown to them, another animal was also present, and it, too, was intent on filling its stomach. A big, catlike creature was lying hidden in the tall grass at the edge of the water hole, motionless except for a nervous twitching of its tail. The cat was much like a tiger in shape, but was more heavily built, and the gently waving tail was shorter and stubbier than that of a tiger.

There was another difference, too. When a tiger's mouth is closed, its teeth can't be seen. This big cat's mouth was closed, but two of its teeth were distinctly visible. Curving down out of the cat's upper lip, on each side of its mouth, were 6-inch-long, wickedly sharp fangs. They were slightly flattened and curved, and resembled nothing so much as the old-fashioned kind of sword called a saber. Running down the length of the backs of those fangs were tiny serrations like the teeth on a saw.

Eyes fixed unwaveringly on the water hole, the saber-toothed cat waited patiently. The ambush was perfect. The cat was completely hidden and the wind was blowing toward it from the water hole, so that no scent could be detected by any animal passing in front of the hiding place.

But the cat was detected—from above. A shadow flickered over the saber-tooth's body as a big vulture wheeled overhead. The bird sailed to the branch of a nearby tree, closed its wings, and perched with long, scrawny neck thrust forward. From the air the vulture had seen the big cat lying in

SMILODON

Mastodon

Giant Vulture

ambush. The vulture had learned early that it had only to stay near such flesh eaters and it, too, would eventually have food —the remains of the flesh eater's kill. So with a patience that matched that of the saber-tooth, the vulture waited.

A group of camels came down to the water hole to drink. When the cat saw them, its tail moved a little faster, but it made no attempt to attack. It could run fast only for a short distance, and by the time it launched itself into a charge, the fleet-footed camels would be galloping to safety. The saber-tooth wanted slower prey, which it could leap on and dispatch quickly. It continued to wait.

Time passed. Then, a measured tread shook the ground. Some big, heavy—and slow—creatures were approaching the water hole.

They were mastodons, a small herd of great, gray animals with enormous curved tusks. And one of them was a calf.

The adult mastodons waded into the water, dunking their trunks and sucking water into them, then coiling their trunks up to squirt water into their open mouths. But the calf wasn't yet interested in quenching its thirst. It strayed a little distance from the others, trunk questing here and there in the tall grass. Perhaps it smelled something, or perhaps it had seen something that made it curious. The little mastodon took a step, then another. Each step brought it closer to the motionless, hidden cat.

Abruptly, as if losing interest, the calf turned to rejoin the herd. As it did so, the saber-tooth rose smoothly to its feet and took two bounds that brought it smashing down onto the calf's back. The cat's mouth opened—not the way a modern lion or tiger's mouth opens, but in a tremendous gape, with the lower jaw dropping straight down and back, nearly flat against the throat. Like a striking snake, the cat's head stabbed down, burying the long, saberlike teeth in the young mastodon's neck. With a single squeal of shock, the calf crumpled onto its side in the grass.

From the water hole there was a trumpeted scream of fury. Several of the mastodons had witnessed the attack on the calf, and they came charging out of the water, trunks curled back over their heads, eyes blazing. The cat whirled and streaked for safety, zigzagging through the grass with the great beasts thudding in pursuit. They chased it for several hundred yards, then one slowed to a stop and turned back, and the others followed.

The calf lay unmoving, blood welling up from the horrible wounds in its neck and staining the grass crimson. Slowly, the herd gathered around the slain youngster. Several of the mastodons eased their trunks under its body as if trying to lift it back onto its feet and coax it to return to life.

Staying under cover, the saber-tooth slunk back to within 50 or 60 yards of the mastodons and lay down in the grass, watching them. For several hours, the mastodons stayed near the dead calf, rocking their big bodies from side to side, uttering rumbles and squeals. Finally, with the afternoon sun low and red in the sky, they turned and trailed away as if admitting at last that the calf was truly dead and there was nothing they could do.

The saber-tooth watched them carefully, but they paid it no further attention. When they were well in the distance, the cat rose to its feet and paced to the body. It began feeding. From the tree, the vulture, which had been joined by others, watched.

When the cat had filled itself to satisfaction, it padded to the water hole and drank noisily, taking in big gulps of water with a ribbonlike tongue. Then, turning away, it prowled off in search of a place to sleep. It would sleep for many hours and awaken hungry to hunt again for another meal. Such was the way of its life.

As the saber-tooth moved away from its kill, the vultures rose from the trees with a great clamor and rustle and swept toward the carcass. Now it was their turn to eat.

The saber-toothed cat has been named *Smilodon*, which means "knife tooth." It lived from about 1 million years ago until about 20 thousand years ago.

Was it much like a modern lion or tiger? It was about the same size, but it was a heavier and probably slower animal. Because of the size of its brain, some scientists think it was not as intelligent as a modern lion, tiger, or even a house cat. Others think it probably was.

Did it have a mane? Was it striped like a tiger, or spotted like a leopard? There's no way to tell, for sure. And was it really the terrible killer that its saberlike teeth seem to indicate? Many scientists think so, but some aren't so sure. They think it may have lived mainly on the bodies of dead animals that it happened to find, just as vultures do.

Whatever its way of life, Smilodon and other saber-toothed cats like it were widespread throughout the world. But by about 20 thousand years ago, they had all become extinct. There are no saber-toothed cats anywhere in the world today.

Present-day Sloth

Megatherium — THE GIANT SLOTH

IN THE FORESTS of South America there lives a little animal called a sloth. Its body is covered with shaggy fur, and its ears and tail are so tiny they can't even be seen. On all four of its feet are long, curling claws, like hooks, that fit neatly around tree branches. The sloth spends nearly its whole life upside down, hanging by its claws from branches, moving along each branch with incredible slowness as it feeds on leaves and buds. From its blunt nose to the invisible tail, the sloth is only about 2 feet long.

About 30 thousand years ago there was another kind of sloth living in South America and the southernmost part of North America. A relative of the little tree sloth, it lived on the ground instead of up in trees. And it wasn't just 2 feet long; it was as big as an elephant! Because of its size, this sloth of long ago has been named *Megatherium*, meaning "giant beast."

Unlike the nearly tailless little tree sloth, Megatherium had a long, enormously thick tail that tapered to a blunt point. But in most other ways the giant sloth was quite a bit like its tiny, modern relative. It, too, had long, curling claws on its feet. But because of those claws it couldn't put its feet down flat when it walked; it lumbered along on

the knuckles of its front feet and the sides of its back ones. This probably caused it to shuffle clumsily.

Like its relative, Megatherium was also covered with shaggy fur. But beneath the fur, imbedded in its skin, were many knobby "pebbles" of bone. This was a kind of armor that somewhat protected the giant sloth from flesh eaters. For in spite of its size, Megatherium was probably often preyed upon by the savage saber-toothed cats that prowled in parts of the world at that time. The sloth was not completely helpless against these marauders, however, for while it used its claws mainly for digging and for pulling tree branches to its mouth, they were also vicious weapons. A single swing of one of those big, clawed paws smashing against an enemy's body would have crunched bones and left terrible, bloody wounds.

Much of what we know about Megatherium was learned from fossil skeletons of the big animal. Many Megatherium bones, together with hundreds of thousands of bones of other mammals and birds, have been taken out of the famous La Brea tar pits, near Los Angeles, California. These tar pits formed millions of years ago by

40

oil that oozed up out of the ground to make sticky pools of tar. They have been death traps for countless thousands of creatures.

We can easily imagine how a megathere might become a victim of the tar pits. On a morning 30 thousand years ago, the sun rose redly over a countryside of broad, grassy plains dotted with clumps of trees and bushes. It glinted on the dew-covered, golden-brown fur of the enormous, shaggy beast that lay sleeping, curled into a great ball in the middle of a grove of trees.

A fly, roused to activity by the morning warmth, buzzed to rest on the megathere's nose. After a moment, the big animal's nostrils twitched and its eyes blinked open. The fly darted away.

The sloth's mouth gaped open in a huge yawn. Then it snorted, and lurching to its feet, ambled off, nose close to the ground in search of an interesting smell that had suddenly caught its attention. It paused where the smell was strongest and began to dig with its claws. Shortly, it uncovered the tasty roots of a clump of wild onions and began to munch on them with immense satisfaction.

After it finished, and when no more interesting smells could be detected, the megathere turned back toward the grove of trees. Making its way to the nearest tree, it suddenly reared up, supporting its weight on its back legs and thick, muscular tail. In this position, its head was among the lower branches of the tree, a good 15 feet off the ground. Reaching up, it hooked its claws around a branch and began to feed. Its long, tubular tongue stretched forth and,

almost like a tentacle, wrapped itself around clusters of leaves, stripping them from the branch and carrying them into the sloth's mouth.

The sloth fed for nearly an hour, moving from one tree to another. At last it was satisfied and dropped its front legs back onto the ground with a thump. Then, with its peculiar waddling walk, it shuffled off across the grassy landscape.

The plain abounded with many kinds of animals, but the hulking sloth ignored them, as they did it. It passed a large herd of zebralike animals grazing placidly, and a little later encountered a small group of mammoths. Once, it passed within a few yards of a saber-toothed cat that had recently fed and lay sleeping, hidden by the tall grass. Had the cat been awake and hungry, the sloth might have been in for trouble.

The sun was high in the sky now, flooding the plain with heat, and the sloth began to feel thirsty. It quickened its pace, turning its big head from side to side, searching for the telltale gleam of water. After a time, as it crossed a slight rise in the ground, it caught sight of a large sheet of silver, sparkling enticingly in the sunlight.

Near the water there was a peculiar tang in the air, a sharp, unfamiliar, oily smell. It was not the smell of an animal, so it meant nothing to the sloth. The big beast merely snorted, to clear the acrid odor from its nostrils, and plodded to the edge of the water, its feet sinking squishily into the ground.

The water at the edge of the pool was

just a thin film, so the sloth moved farther out. With each step its feet sank deeper, and it was harder to pull them loose. Suddenly, the sloth couldn't move at all! The pool of water was really a deep pool of black, sticky tar, covered with only a thin coat of oily water.

Not understanding what was happening to it, the megathere tried to pull first one foot loose, then another. Its movements only made it sink deeper, until its legs and belly were completely immersed in the treacherous tar. Completely helpless, the big beast suddenly sensed its terrible predicament and began to wallow in panic, straining its body and making terrified noises.

Soon, only the sloth's head was above the tar. Its eyes rolled wildly, and it stretched its neck, desperately trying to snatch a few more seconds of life. But the very weight of its own big body continued to pull it down. Slowly, its head went under. Tar filled its nose and mouth and death came quickly.

The sloth's body continued to sink into the sticky blackness, and after a time its skin and flesh rotted away. Thirty thousand or more years after its death, its bones, and those of many other animals, were discovered by workmen as they were removing tar from the pit to use for paving roads.

Our knowledge of giant sloths doesn't all come from just their bones, however. In a cave in South America and in caves in North America's Southwest, fragments of the skin and hair of giant sloths have been found, marvelously preserved by the dry air. From these fragments, scientists learned about the color and texture of Megatherium's fur, and about the pebbly, bone armor that was imbedded in its skin.

Those fragments of skin and hair also told us something else—that giant sloths have not been extinct for very long. Scientists feel sure that these huge, shaggy, elephant-sized animals of the prehistoric world were still lumbering about in South America no more than a few hundred years ago!

But today, the only sloths in South America are the little 2-foot-long tree sloths, hanging upside down among the leafy branches.

Glyptodon — A MAMMAL WITH A SHELL

ONE MILLION years ago, a great grassy plain covered much of the southern part of South America. It was almost as flat and even as a tabletop, stretching away on all sides under a wide open sky. Giant thistles grew thickly among the pampas grass, and their pale, purple flowers, nodding above the grass tops, made the plain look as if it were coated with a lavender haze. When the wind blew, the tall tassels of grass and the spiky heads of the thistles swirled and swayed, so that whole sections of the land seemed to be running away in front of the breeze.

The late afternoon sun hung low in the sky over the great plain, tinting it orange and casting patches of purple shadow. The vast carpet of grass appeared to be empty of life. But abruptly, there was movement. Something rose up out of the grass and began to follow a slow zigzag course with many pauses. From a distance it looked like nothing so much as a big, dome-shaped boulder lurching through the grass all by itself!

It was an animal whose body was covered with a great, humped, turtlelike shell. It was not a turtle, however, for its small, roundish head and the portions of its feet that peeped out from under the shell were furry—a sure sign that the beast was a mammal. It was about 9 feet long from nose to tail, and its shell was nearly 4 feet high. Its legs were stout, with short, stubby toes and thick, blunt claws. It was an animal that has been named *Glyptodon*.

An enormous number of animals swarmed through the vast sea of grass where Glyptodon lived. For most of them, life was simply a matter of keeping one leap ahead of some other animal's hungry mouth, for they were all part of the great food chain of the grassland. By the millions, tiny, many-legged creatures—the insects that crawled and hunted and fed and laid their eggs among the stalks of grass—became food for other insects, for birds, and for little mouselike mammals. And those animals, in their turn, were preyed on by snakes, larger birds, and larger mammals. Not even the biggest animals could escape from the food chain. The huge, shaggy, elephant-sized sloths that shuffled ponderously about on the plain were often pulled down by the tigerlike saber-toothed cats that prowled through the grass. The toxodonts—short-legged, big-headed animals that looked somewhat like 9-foot-long

44

Toxodon

guinea pigs with tusks—were prized food for many hungry flesh eaters.

But chances are that Glyptodon did not have much to fear from other creatures. It was not a fierce animal that could defend itself with sharp teeth and claws, and it certainly wasn't a swift runner, able to outdistance the flesh eaters, but it was well protected by its bony shell. Also, it had a "secret weapon."

Glyptodon was a relative of the animals called armadillos that live today in South and Central America and in the southern part of North America. There are several kinds of armadillos, but they all have bony shells covering their bodies. These shells aren't stiff, like turtle shells; they're movable. One kind of armadillo can curl itself up when it is in danger, tucking its tail, paws, and nose into its shell. This turns it into a hard, bony ball that most animals cannot bite. Another kind of armadillo can quickly dig itself into the ground and wedge itself in so that nothing is exposed but its hard, bone-covered back.

But Glyptodon did not use either of these two methods of defense. It had what may have been a better way of defending itself. Its shell was thick and stiff and rock-hard; it had a kind of "helmet" of thick bone on the top of its head; and its thick, heavy tail was covered with knobby bumps of bone. So when Glyptodon was in danger it simply crouched down and lowered its head. Its feet were then covered completely by the shell, and the only part of its head that showed was the part covered by the bony cap. In this position, Glyptodon was noth-

ing but a big, round dome of rock-hard bone—not at all the sort of thing that a saber-toothed cat or a wolf would want to sink its fangs into.

Of course, Glyptodon's bone-covered tail was not covered by the shell. And that hard tail was Glyptodon's secret weapon—a war club. Glyptodon could swing it, suddenly and savagely, to smash it into the body of a wolf or cat that was snuffling about too closely. One kind of Glyptodon even had a big cluster of sharp, bony spikes on the tip of its tail, like the war club called a mace that knights of long ago used in their battles.

With its bony armor shell, Glyptodon was, of course, very much like a turtle. It was also a lot like another kind of animal that had lived many millions of years earlier, a dinosaur called *Ankylosaurus*. Ankylosaurus, too, was covered with bony armor and had a knobby, spiky tail that it could use as a war club. Yet Glyptodon was not at all closely related to either of these two creatures. Turtles are reptiles. Ankylosaurus was also. Glyptodon was, of course, a mammal. But they are all so much alike that it's easy to see how Nature often repeats ways of helping living things take care of themselves.

What did Glyptodon eat, and what sort of life did it live? It belonged to the group of animals called "edentates," a group that includes armadillos, sloths, and anteaters. *Edentata* means "without teeth," but actually, most of these animals do have teeth, although their teeth are often nothing more than rather weak pegs. Glyptodon's teeth

46

Doedicurus

show that it couldn't have been a flesh eater but perhaps it wasn't just a plant eater, either. Its relatives, the armadillos, eat lots of insects, grubs, and worms, and a few kinds of berries, so perhaps Glyptodon's diet was somewhat like theirs.

Glyptodon probably didn't live the same sort of life that its armadillo cousins do, though. Most armadillos are great diggers and make burrows for themselves in which they hide and sleep. But Glyptodon's blunt claws must not have been much good for digging, and with its stiff, turtlelike shell it wouldn't have been able to move around in a burrow very easily. Glyptodon may have just wandered about on the grasslands and the edges of deserts, looking for the things it ate and squatting down inside its armored shell whenever it encountered a flesh-eating animal that began to show too much hungry interest in it.

Glyptodon seems to have started out in South America about 50 million years ago.

At first it was a little creature, much like an armadillo, but as millions of years passed, it got bigger and bigger and its movable, armadillolike shell changed into a stiff, bony dome. By about 1 million years ago, this large, bony-armored animal was living in the grasslands and prairies throughout South and Central America and the southern parts of North America.

Despite its long history and apparently successful way of defending itself, Glyptodon became extinct by about 25 thousand years ago. It left no descendants or relatives of any kind. Fortunately there are still armadillos in the world to help us understand what kind of an animal Glyptodon was, for otherwise this unusual beast would have posed a real problem for scientists. Except for the armadillos, no mammal living today has bony armor on its body. So who could have imagined a creature such as Glyptodon—a furry mammal in a turtle shell!

Present-day Armadillo

Mammoth — THE FURRY ELEPHANT

THE LAND was flat and gray-green beneath a sullen gray sky. A biting wind rushed over the ground, rattling the few stunted bushes that huddled here and there on the landscape. It was autumn on the tundra, the great barren plain that lies between the ever-frozen north polar lands and the huge evergreen forest that stretches across the northern part of the world. Soon, the ground that had thawed to a depth of a few inches during the brief spring and summer would be frozen ironhard again and covered with a heavy, white blanket of snow.

Out of the northern horizon came a cluster of dark, shaggy shapes. They moved with ponderous majesty, heads nodding, trunks curling and uncurling. They were very much like modern elephants, but their backs and heads were higher and rounder, and their ears much smaller than those of an elephant. And they were completely covered with thick, reddish-brown hair. They were mammoths.

It was a small herd of only seven adults and two young calves. The calves looked like fat, fuzzy balls, and their tusks were still short and only slightly curved. The tusks of the older beasts formed great C-shaped curves. In winter, those thick, curved tusks helped the mammoths get their food. When the animals lowered their heads and rolled them from side to side, their curved tusks scooped away the snow, enabling them to reach the grass and moss beneath.

But food was no problem, yet. As the mammoths plodded along in their slow, stately fashion, their hairy trunks coiled down to pluck up herbs, flowers, clumps of moss, and tufts of grass. The tips of their trunks, which of course were their noses, were much like modern elephants' trunks. There was a kind of muscular "finger" above the nostrils and a thick flap below that could be used almost like a hand.

The leader of the herd, a 10-foot-tall male, came to the steep bank of a stream. He turned aside, following the course of the stream toward the great fir forest that loomed like a dim green cloud far in the distance on the southern horizon. Silently, the others swung into line behind him, the two calves close to their mothers.

For many years, the river bank at this point had been crumbling away as the melting snow each spring had swollen the stream, turning it for a time into a swift-

48

moving flood. Now, a large section of the bank was ready to collapse entirely. And it was on this section that the last mammoth in the line, a young male, chanced to put his full weight.

Suddenly, the bank gave way beneath him. He dropped like a stone, 20 feet into the shallow water and mud of the stream, landing in a sitting position with a smashing shock that broke his hip and right foreleg. A torrent of mud and icy earth poured down around him as a great section of the bank collapsed completely. The mammoth had time for only a quick squeal of pain and terror before he was completely buried under several tons of muck.

He struggled in panic, but the soft mud held him, and his broken bones would not permit him to move. Unable to fight his way free, he was dead of suffocation in minutes.

The young mammoth's squeal had startled the rest of the herd. They stopped short at the sound, then quickly bunched together, peering about for signs of danger and emitting rumbles and squeals of worry. Their eyesight was not very keen, but their sense of smell was excellent, and it told them no other animals were nearby. But they sensed that something had happened and were puzzled and disturbed by the disappearance of one of their companions. The old leader pointed his trunk into the air and screamed out a call. Then, dropping his trunk, he stood shifting his big body from side to side as if anxiously awaiting an answer.

After several minutes he seemed to come to a decision, and turning, plodded once more on his way. The others followed. But from time to time one of them would break stride and swing around to trumpet shrilly, as if seeking sight or sound of the missing young male. Worried and uneasy, the animals moved on toward the distant forest, leaving far behind them the river bank where the young mammoth lay buried.

Days passed. The sky grew ever darker and the wind more piercingly cold. The ground began to freeze. In a few weeks it was frozen stone-cold beneath a cover of white snow. And the mammoth's body, in its tomb of ice and earth, was frozen as hard as the ground.

The mammoth lay on the edge of the flood plain near the riverbed, and the bank of the river sloped up more than 20 feet above it. When spring came, melting snow and falling rain washed more dirt down the bank. Some of this was carried away by the river, but some of it piled up on the mammoth's grave, burying the animal deeper. In the cold earth, its body stayed frozen.

Each year, for centuries, more of the river bank eroded away, slipping down to lie on top of the mammoth's grave. Finally, the bank was gone. And with it out of the way, the wind and water were now free to begin their work of eroding the mammoth's grave, carrying dirt away from it a little at a time. After many thousands of springs, the mammoth's body, which had once been deeply buried, was close to the surface.

In the spring of 1900, torrential rains fell, washing away the thawing soil and uncovering frozen soil that thawed and was washed away in its turn. The mammoth's body was uncovered.

In August of that year, a hunter by the name of Semen Tarabykin, with his dog, was tracking an elk near the Berezovka River, in Siberia. Abruptly, the dog swerved, racing off in excitement after a strange, new scent. The dog led Tarabykin to a huge, shaggy body that looked as if it were just crawling out of the earth.

That was the beginning of one of the greatest episodes in the science of zoology. Slowly, word was carried out of the remote Siberian wilderness that the perfectly preserved body of a creature that had vanished from the earth thousands of years before had been discovered.

In May of 1901, when the news reached the Academy of Sciences in St. Petersburg (now called Leningrad), Russia, an expedition set out at once. After a dreadfully difficult journey, the Russian scientists reached the mammoth's body in September.

The body had begun to decay. Worse still, wolves and bears, attracted by the smell, had gnawed away portions of it. At once the scientists began the task of digging the body out of the frozen ground, skinning it, and examining its parts.

The mammoth was a scientific treasure trove. The men found that beneath its long, shaggy hair, it was covered with soft, yellowish fur, like wool, that had helped keep it warm even in the fiercest cold. In its stomach and between its teeth they found remains of the food it had eaten the very day it died. And they found that meat on its back legs was still fresh, tempting them to cook some of the meat and try it. Imagine eating the kind of meat that cavemen had eaten many thousands of years before! But, fearful, they fed it instead to their dogs who gobbled it up gladly.

By mid-October, the work was finished and the expedition returned to St. Petersburg. In the Museum of the Academy of Sciences, the body of the mammoth was stuffed and mounted in exactly the same position it was in when found.

Skeletons of other mammoths, and even portions of mammoths' bodies with skin and fur still on them, have been found in other places since then, for mammoths once lived all over Europe and North America. But it was the Berezovka mammoth that taught us much of what we now know about these ancient members of the elephant family, and that is still regarded as one of the greatest scientific finds of this century.

URSUS SPELAEUS (CAVE BEAR)

Ursus Spelaeus — THE GREAT CAVE BEAR

HIGH AMONG the limestone cliffs that overlooked a winding river, a blob of darkness marked the entrance to a cave. Far back within the cave, in a corner where a thin trickle of cold water seeped out of a crack in the limestone, lay a mother cave bear and two cubs.

The mother bear was a big shaggy beast more than 9 feet long and nearly 5 feet high at the shoulders. Her head was massive, and the front part of her body was more powerfully built, and higher, than the back part. When she yawned, she showed the sharp, savage teeth of a meat eater. Yet she ate not only the flesh of animals, but a great many other types of food, as well—berries, nuts, many kinds of leafy plants, insects, seeds. Much of the meat she ate came from the bodies of dead animals she found, which undoubtedly included the giant deer and the woolly rhinoceros. Much food was also provided by many kinds of small creatures such as ground squirrels, frogs, lizards, and fish. But she could also hunt and bring down many larger animals, such as deer and goats.

The mother bear was nervous. For several minutes she had been aware of strange sounds and smells coming from outside the cave. They were unfamiliar sounds and smells, and there was something about them she didn't like. Her lip twitched back in a snarl.

The cave bear didn't know it, but she who had so often been a hunter was now herself being hunted. Her den had been discovered by a party of men searching for food or shelter, and the sounds and smells were coming from them as they made their preparations outside the cave.

These men were short, powerfully built humans with rugged features. In nearly 90 thousands years, when the bones of their kind would first be discovered in a valley in France, they would become known as Neanderthal men. They knew how to make fire and how to make tools and weapons of flaked flint. They probably wore animal-skin garments and spoke a simple language. And they were skillful hunters of the great cave bears.

The bear rose to her feet and paced a few steps forward. A sharp, biting smell was drifting into the cave now. She growled.

Suddenly, a terrific noise broke out outside the cave. The Neanderthal men were shouting at the top of their lungs. Half a dozen flaming branches were hurled into

Giant Deer

Woolly Rhinoceros

the cave to lie crackling on the rocky floor, filling the cave with acrid, stinging smoke. The bear snarled. The shouts alarmed and excited her and the flaring torches frightened her. The smoke made her eyes smart and her throat burn. She sensed danger to her cubs from all this sudden noise and activity, and when a she-bear's cubs are threatened, her instincts give her only one course of action. She charges.

With a savage roar, the huge beast rushed out of the cave. Instantly she was pelted with a furious barrage of big, sharp-edged, heavy rocks, hurled down on her by a score of men who had taken positions among the high boulders around the cave's entrance. Ahead of her, a ring of fires blocked her path, and behind them a row of men leaped, howled, and waved burning branches.

Hurt and confused, the bear stopped short, snarling. More rocks rained down on her. One smashed into her head, opening a great cut. Another ripped a deep gash in her back. Thrown torches singed her fur.

Roaring with pain and fury, the bear whirled, trying to get at her attackers, but they were out of reach. A boulder crashed against her snout, blinding her with pain. Whimpering, she dropped into a crouch. One man, more daring than the others, leaped down and drove a spear into her side—a long, straight tree branch that had been sharpened at one end and hardened in fire. With a roar of pain, the bear swung toward him, but he scrambled back up among the boulders.

The bear began to weaken. Bleeding from a score of gashes, bruised and dazed by the rocks that continued to pelt her, and with the spear jutting from her side, her movements grew slower. Grasping their spears firmly, the Neanderthal men began to slip down out of the boulders and close in.

Finally, the great bear lay dead. The Neanderthals clustered about her, gazing at the huge, shaggy form. One man sat gasping on the ground, clutching a gashed arm that had been ripped open by a final swipe of the bear's paw.

One of the men happened to glance toward the cave entrance and gave a grunt, alerting the others. The bear cubs, puzzled and frightened at having been left alone, had worked up their courage to follow their mother and were emerging timidly from the cave. Quickly, several of the hunters moved toward them, and quickly, the cubs joined their mother. The Neanderthals lived in a harsh world where food was often hard to find, and they had little ones of their own to feed. To them, the cubs simply represented more food.

Now the work of skinning and cutting up the great bear began. But first, there was something important the Neanderthals had to do. With their surprisingly sharp stone tools they hacked off the bear's head. Then several of them, one carrying the big head, set out to climb far up to a point near the top of the mountain where there was another cave.

At the cave entrance they lit torches and trooped silently into the gloomy interior. Inside there were several caves connected by narrow passageways. In the passageway between the second and third caves the men halted and piled their torches together on the rocky floor.

The flames flickered redly against a pile of stone slabs that lay at the opening of the third cave. Two of the Neanderthals began to remove slabs from the top of the pile. Shortly, the firelight revealed several gleaming white objects around which the slabs had been placed. These objects were skulls—the skulls of cave bears. Stepping forward, the man who carried the head of the bear that had just been killed placed it among the skulls.

This pile of rocks and cave bear skulls that was made so long ago by Neanderthal hunters was discovered by modern scientists in the cave at the top of Dragon Mountain, in Austria. What *was* the pile? An altar? A place of sacrifice? Did the Neanderthal men worship the great bears they hunted and put the skulls in this place as an act of respect? Or were the bear skulls put there as a sacrifice of thanksgiving to a god that had helped the Neanderthals have a successful hunt? We shall probably never know, but it is certain that cave bears were of great importance to the Neanderthal

people, both as a source of food and as objects of some strange religious or magical ceremony.

The great cave bear hunted by our Neanderthal ancestors has a relative that looks very much like it living today. It is the North American grizzly bear. In fact, skeletons of the prehistoric cave bear and the modern grizzly are so much alike that many experts think the grizzly is the cave bear's descendant. It is believed that the grizzly's cave bear ancestors might have come to North America at the same time as the ancestors of the Indians, traveling across the bridge of land that connected North America and Asia during the late Ice Age.

Sadly enough, this beast that is so much like its prehistoric ancestor may soon be just as extinct as most of the long-ago mammals of the Ice Age. For the grizzly bear is vanishing. Where there once were hundreds of thousands of grizzlies, there are now probably less than 20 thousand, and their numbers grow less each year. So one of the last links with the prehistoric world that can still be seen and studied is following the saber-toothed cat and the mammoth down the road that leads to extinction.

Baluchitherium — THE BIGGEST OF ALL

BENEATH A tall tree, a tiny ratlike animal had found an overripe fruit that had fallen to the ground and was devouring it with great enjoyment. The tree stood at the edge of a large thicket that was one of many such clusters of trees and shrubs dotting an immense, grassy plain.

As the ratlike creature daintily nibbled at its repast with quick little bites, it suddenly became aware of a sensation coming from the ground beneath its feet. The earth was shaking with short, sharp quivers, each quiver accompanied by the thud of a huge, heavy foot. For a moment, the little creature froze into a crouch. Then, as a huge shape loomed over it, the tiny beast whipped out of sight around the broad tree trunk and scurried to safety.

The animal that had come to the tree and startled the little ratlike thing away from its meal of fruit was enormous. An automobile could have driven between its legs and never touched either its knees or its stomach. The creature's great, bulky body was 18 feet high at the shoulders and 34 feet long—more than twice as long and half again as high as most elephants! The weight of its big feet, thudding on the earth as it walked, had made the ground shake.

Its gigantic head, as long as a man's whole body, was set on a long neck that reached easily into the upper branches of the tree, nearly 25 feet above the ground.

The beast began to browse. It had two large teeth projecting downward from the front of its upper jaw, with which it stripped great clusters of leaves from the branches in a single motion. It chewed the leaves with back teeth the size of apples— big by our standards, but small for so large a beast.

Shortly, the huge animal was joined by several others. These creatures lived in small herds, roaming from thicket to thicket on the vast plain, always in search of food. They were hearty eaters, for it took a lot of leaves to keep those big bodies going.

What were these giant creatures—dinosaurs? Not at all. While they were certainly as big as some of the large dinosaurs, they were nevertheless mammals—the biggest mammals that have ever walked on the earth. They lived about 20 million years ago, on the great plain that covered central Asia. Because their bones were discovered in the part of Asia called Baluchistan, these giant mammals were named *Baluchitherium* —the "Beast of Baluchistan."

For a long time, no one knew exactly what kind of creature the Beast of Baluchistan was. A few of its neck bones and leg bones were discovered in 1911 by an English scientist. He could tell they were the bones of a mammal, but what kind of mammal could have been so gigantic?

It took 11 years to find out. In 1922, a party of American scientists in the Gobi Desert of central Asia discovered some enormous teeth and leg bones that they identified as belonging to Baluchitherium. And a few days later, digging in the same place, they uncovered a portion of a gigantic skull. From that skull they were able to tell exactly what mammal family the beast belonged to. It was a giant rhinoceros! A giant rhinoceros without horns!

Actually, Baluchitherium was a kind of cousin of the rhinoceroses that live now, and not their ancestor. Long ago, probably more than 50 million years ago, there was apparently a split in the rhino family. Some kinds of rhinos began to get larger and grow horns in order to protect themselves. Another kind of rhino never developed horns, but it, too, got larger—and larger and *larger*—and finally evolved into the giant Baluchitherium. Since size can be as much protection for an animal as horns, the chances are that the giant Beast of Baluchistan was quite safe from flesh eaters, even though it had no horns. Probably not even a saber-toothed cat would have risked get-

ting trampled by such a monster.

Baluchitherium roamed the grassy plains of central Asia for several million years. The climate was warm, and there were plenty of trees from which it could get food. Then, slowly, the great range of Himalaya Mountains was pushed up by earthquakes and volcanic action. After many thousands of years the mountains were high enough to act like a great wall, blocking out the warm, rain-filled winds that had kept the great plain green and fertile. The grassy plain began to dry up. It became the desert it is today. And the giant, hornless rhinos all died out.

The prehistoric world was full of big, strange beasts, and Baluchitherium was certainly the king of them all. But of all those giants of long ago, only the big, gray elephant, and Baluchitherium's smaller relative, the rhinoceros, are left to give us an inkling of what some of the animals of that ancient world were like. There isn't much room for giant animals anymore, in a world filled with mankind's towns and cities. But as we look at the awesome skeletons of such creatures as the Beast of Baluchistan, we cannot help but wonder if, sometime in the far future when the Age of Mammals has come to an end, just as the Age of Reptiles did, the earth may not once more feel the footsteps of strange, giant creatures about which we can now only guess.

Pronunciation Guide

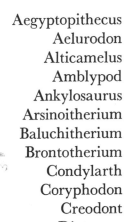

Aegyptopithecus	(ee-JIP-tuh-PITH-ik-uhs)
Aelurodon	(ee-LYUR-uh-dahn)
Alticamelus	(AL-tih-kuh-MEE-luhs)
Amblypod	(AM-blih-pahd)
Ankylosaurus	(ANG-kih-loh-SAW-ruhs)
Arsinoitherium	(AHR-sih-noy-THEE-rih-uhm)
Baluchitherium	(buh-LOO-chih-THEE-rih-uhm)
Brontotherium	(BRAHN-toh-THEE-rih-uhm)
Condylarth	(KAHN-dih-lahrth)
Coryphodon	(koh-RIF-oh-dahn)
Creodont	(KREE-oh-dahnt)
Diatryma	(DY-uh-TRY-muh)
Doedicurus	(dee-DIH-kyu-ruhs)
Edentate	(ee-DEN-tayt)
Eohippus	(EE-oh-HIP-uhs)
Glyptodon	(GLIP-toh-dahn)
Hyaenodon	(hy-EE-noh-dahn)
Hyracotherium	(HY-ruh-koh-THEE-rih-uhm)
Hyrax	(HY-raks)
Icthyornis	(ik-thee-AWR-nehs)
Mammoth	(MAM-uhth)
Megatherium	(MEG-uh-THEE-rih-uhm)
Merychippus	(MER-ih-KIP-uhs)
Mesohippus	(MES-oh-HIP-uhs)
Moeritherium	(MEH-rih-THEE-rih-uhm)
Neanderthal	(nee-AN-der-thahl)
Orohippus	(AWR-oh-HIP-uhs)
Oxyeana	(ahx-ee-EE-nuh)
Phenacodus	(fee-NAK-oh-duhs)
Platybelodon	(plat-ee-BEL-oh-dahn)
Poëbrotherium	(POH-uh-broh-THEE-rih-uhm)
Procamelus	(PROH-kuh-MEE-luhs)
Smilodon	(SMY-loh-dahn)
Titanotherium	(TY-tan-oh-THEE-rih-uhm)
Toxodon	(TAHK-soh-dahn)

Index